BURIED ALIVE!

HOW 33 MINERS SURVIVED 69 DAYS DEEP UNDER THE CHILEAN DESERT

ELAINE SCOTT

CLARION BOOKS ▪ HOUGHTON MIFFLIN HARCOURT ▪ BOSTON NEW YORK

TO THE THIRTY-THREE MINERS

Clarion Books
215 Park Avenue South
New York, New York 10003

The text of this book is set in 15-point Baily Sans.
Map and diagrams by Lloyd Miller

Clarion Books is an imprint of Houghton Mifflin Harcourt Publishing Company.

www.hmhbooks.com

Library of Congress Cataloging-in-Publication Data
Scott, Elaine, 1940–
Buried alive! : how 33 miners survived 69 days deep under the Chilean desert / by Elaine Scott.
p. cm.
ISBN 978-0-547-70778-5
1. San José Mine Accident, Chile, 2010—Juvenile literature. 2. Gold mines and mining—Accidents—Chile—Copiapó Region
—Juvenile literature. 3. Copper mines and mining—Accidents—Chile—Copiapó Region—Juvenile literature. 4. Mine rescue
work—Chile—Copiapó Region—Juvenile literature. I. Title.
TN311.S43 2012
363.11'962234220983145—dc23
2011025945

Manufactured in China
SCP 10 9 8 7 6 5 4 3
4500422546

Please note the photographs of the miners inside the mine are stills taken from video.

(previous page) A truck carrying miners travels along the road from Copiapó, Chile, to the San José mine. REUTERS

AND THOSE WHO WORKED, WAITED, AND WORRIED

No man is an island, entire of itself; every man is a piece of the continent, a part of the main; if a clod be washed away by the sea, Europe is the less, as well as if a promontory were, as well as if a manor of thy friend's or of thine own were; any man's death diminishes me, because I am involved in mankind; and therefore never send to know for whom the bell tolls; it tolls for thee.

—John Donne, "Meditation XVII"

UNTIL THEY WERE FINALLY FREE

ACKNOWLEDGMENTS

Because the story of the miners and their rescue has so many important themes, I knew I had to record it for today's young readers and for those yet to come. I am grateful to my agent, Susan Cohen of Writers House, and my editor at Clarion, Jennifer Greene, who agreed and were early and enthusiastic supporters of this project. During the research, Greg Hall became a wonderful resource for me as well as an inspiration. He read the manuscript for mistakes and offered suggestions, as did my husband, Parker, a man who also knows his way around a drill rig. A heartfelt thanks to each of you.

CONTENTS

INTRODUCTION

ON August 5, 2010, Mario Gómez was preparing to go to work at the San José mine, high in the Atacama Desert of Chile. Mario had worked in the mines since he was twelve years old. He was now sixty-three and ready to retire. And he was worried. A month earlier, Mario had confided to his wife, Lilianet, that he feared parts of the San José were starting to collapse. "Only a little," said Lilianet when she recalled the conversation. "But it was collapsing."

Mario was not the only miner with concerns, and he and his colleagues reported the danger to the San Esteban Mining Company's managers and owners. According to Lilianet, "All the miners knew, but when they spoke to the mine owners, asking them to do something, the bosses said, 'If you don't want to work in the mine, then get up and go. There are four or five others who will happily take your place.'"

The San José mine had already been the scene of countless accidents and had claimed the lives of several miners, including Pedro Gonzalez, who died as the result of a cave-in in 2004. In 2006 Fernando Contreras died in a truck accident,

A road through the Atacama Desert in Chile leading to the San José mine. ASSOCIATED PRESS

and in 2007, Manuel Villagrán was killed by a cascade of loose rocks. Finally, Sernageomin, the Chilean government agency responsible for mine safety, ordered the San José to close until proper safety measures could be taken. Those safety measures were largely ignored, and in 2008 the San José was allowed to reopen.

The entrance to the San José mine was closed after the collapse and barricaded with wire mesh. Police officers patrolled the area regularly. ASSOCIATED PRESS

More disaster followed. In July 2010 another miner, Gino Cortés, was leaving his shift when a large rock fell, crushing his leg and requiring its amputation. Falling rocks are always a danger in a mine, and Cortés claimed the mine was short on the kinds of metal screens that keep loose rocks in their place. About the accident that cost Gino Cortés his leg, Lilianet said, "My husband was involved in that. Afterward I said I wanted him to stop working there, but he convinced me he would carry on until December." So on that August day, Mario left for work as usual.

For some men, the lure of the mines is stronger than any fear of danger. They might be attracted to the job because it is a family tradition and their

Newer employees of the San Esteban Mining Company were not paid as much as those who had worked there longer. Carlos Mamani, from Bolivia, lived in a poor neighborhood outside Copiapó, a small city near the San José mine. Homes in this area often lacked running water and sewers. ASSOCIATED PRESS

work follows in the footsteps of fathers, uncles, brothers, cousins, and friends who were miners. Others are attracted to mining out of national pride. Chile is the world's leading producer of copper, and copper is its chief export. In order to be useful to the world—and to Chile's economy—the copper has to be extracted from the earth, or mined. Chilean miners are proud to be part of the process, proud to contribute to their nation's economic growth.

They are proud to be able to help themselves economically too. A job in a mine like the San José paid an average salary of $940 a month. It's good work for men who have not had an opportunity to finish their education and provides a way out of poverty. The miners who worked in the San José knew it was a dangerous mine, but they believed the reward was worth the risk.

It was worth it to Ariel Ticona, a young father who worked in the San José alongside Mario Gómez. He and his wife, Elizabeth, were parents of two young children, and a third was on the way. Just before he entered the mine shaft on August 5, Ariel made a phone call home. It was 7:00 a.m., and he wanted to be certain Elizabeth was up so she could take their six-year-old son to school.

Mario Gómez and Ariel Ticona were miners. As every miner knows, when he says goodbye to his family and rides down into the ground at the beginning of his shift, there is always a possibility he will not ride out again at the end of the day.

"IF YOU DON'T WANT TO WORK IN THE MINE, THEN GET UP AND GO. THERE ARE FOUR OR FIVE OTHERS WHO WILL HAPPILY TAKE YOUR PLACE."

SURVIVING TOGETHER

Some jobs, like that of an astronaut, are relatively new occupations. People have been flying in space only since April 1, 1961, when the Russian cosmonaut Yuri Gagarin made the first space flight. Other jobs have been around for thousands of years. Mining is one of those ancient jobs. When the earliest humans bent over and picked up pieces of flint lying on the ground and then fashioned the flint into tools—crude knives, or tips for spears—they were mining, taking minerals from the earth. Picking up flint from the ground is a form of surface mining. Surface mining is a broad term that covers any type of mining that does not require digging a shaft into the earth. Strip mining, often used to extract coal, and quarry mining, frequently used to obtain aluminum, are other forms of surface mining. Both types of mining are practiced today. Surface miners use heavy earthmoving equipment like bulldozers and draglines to remove the layers of dirt and rock covering shallow mineral deposits.

But most of Earth's precious minerals—gold, silver, copper, and tin, among many others—are not that easy to find. They are located in deposits called *veins* that lie buried deep within the earth. Mining these veins requires drilling, digging, and descending into darkness in order to extract the mineral-rich deposits, called ore. There are two kinds of underground mines: *shaft mines*, where the opening, or shaft, is vertical to the earth's surface, and *slope mines*, where the opening is drilled at an angle to the ground.

Located near the small city of Copiapó, in the Atacama Desert of northern Chile, the San José is a medium-size slope mine that has produced copper, and some gold, for the past 120 years. Mario Gómez, Ariel Ticona, and their coworkers were mining for copper when they descended about a half mile (a distance almost equal to *two* Empire State Buildings sitting on top of each other) beneath the earth's surface. Early in the morning of August 5, 2010, the men made the trip into the mine in pickup trucks that carried them along the corkscrew-shaped shaft in a twisting journey into the earth. On their way down, they passed through some of the hardest rock in the world.

The descent carried them alongside the vein of copper and past the narrow ventilation shaft that provided fresh air below. The repair shop, where the heavy equipment used in the mine was fixed, lay off the main shaft, in a chamber to the west. The underground-labyrinth world of the San José had been expanded over more than one hundred years of use and now had about five miles of tunnels running off its main shaft. In addition, horizontal passages, called galleries, connected various parts of the mine. At the bottom of the shaft was a small space with benches on either side of it, some stocks of emergency food, and a few first aid supplies. A sign marked it as REFUGIO DE EMERGENCIA, or emergency refuge. This space was intended to provide shelter, food, and safety for the miners in case of danger.

On August 5, thirty-one other men were working the same shift and in

In Alberta, Canada, draglines surface mine for coal by removing layers of earth.
ASSOCIATED PRESS

the same area as Mario and Ariel. Some had worked in the mines for years, others for only a few months. Mario Gómez had been working underground more than fifty years; the youngest member of the group, nineteen-year-old Jimmy Sánchez, had worked in the mine for just five months. All of them were supervised by their foreman, fifty-four-year-old Luis Urzúa, who was affectionately known as Don Lucho.

In Spanish, Lucho is a nickname for Luis. Don is a title of honor in Latin

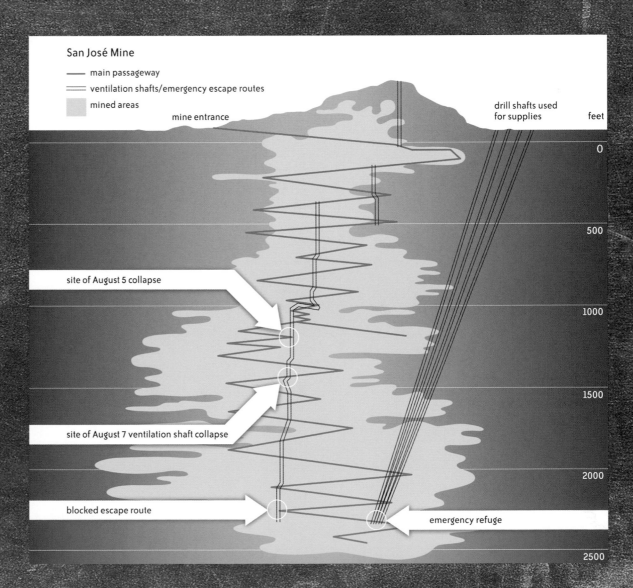

San José Mine

— main passageway

═ ventilation shafts/emergency escape routes

░ mined areas

mine entrance

drill shafts used for supplies

feet

0

500

site of August 5 collapse

1000

site of August 7 ventilation shaft collapse

1500

2000

blocked escape route

emergency refuge

2500

American culture, bestowed on leaders, and Luis Urzúa was a natural leader. According to his mother, he was always a "bossy boots." Even as a child, he took charge, working to help his mother support his five siblings after their stepfather died. As an adult working in the mines, he had earned the respect of his coworkers. Gino Cortés, the miner who had lost his leg in the San José mine a month before, had worked with Luis Urzúa. He said later in reference to the miners, "They were lucky to have a leader like him. He's an exceptional boss."

A good reputation is one of the characteristics of a great leader. A strong leader must also be capable of facing problems head-on and creating viable plans to solve them. On the morning of August 5, 2010, "Bossy Boots" Luis Urzúa was about to face the biggest problem of his life—and of the lives of the thirty-two men in his care.

It happened at 2:00 p.m. local time. There had been weeping—a mining term for intermittent rockfalls and creaking sounds—within the mine for weeks. However, on this day, deep inside the mine but above the level where the men were working, the sounds changed. First there was a rumble, then a sharp, explosive crash.

Television cameras captured the sign deep in the mine that led to the emergency shelter. When the miners arrived at the shelter, they discovered no electricity, little ventilation, and few food supplies. REUTERS

Within the darkness of the mine, Don Lucho gives a "V" for victory. He took charge of his men and tried to remain optimistic. ASSOCIATED PRESS

Chilean mining minister Laurence Golborne addresses the crowd upon his arrival at the San José mine.

The roof of the shaft had collapsed. Mario Gómez described the experience. "That was the most terrible day. In the middle of the cave-in, I thought that we'd never get out of there again. It felt like the mountain was exploding all around us. It cracked. It moved. It stretched like chewing gum. This went on for about twenty minutes." Don Lucho immediately led his men into the shelter of the refuge.

Clouds of thick dust caused by falling rock cascaded down the remains of the shaft, irritating the eyes of the miners below and temporarily blinding some of them. The dust hovered for several hours. When it finally cleared, Luis Urzúa led Mario Sepúlveda, an electrical specialist, and a few others on a scouting mission to identify the extent of their problem and to search for a possible escape route. Don Lucho ordered the remaining men to stay in the refuge. There was always the danger of another collapse, as the badly shaken mine continued to shift under the pressure of the earth.

Luis and Mario Sepúlveda headed up to a ventilation shaft and its safety ladder. It would be a hard climb up 2,300 feet to the surface, but it would be an escape into fresh air, sunshine, and safety. The men tested the ladder and climbed upward. Then, another disaster: the ladder ended after 690 feet, only a third of the way up. It didn't even come close to reaching the surface. The mine owners had left the only escape route incomplete.

The two men had to climb back down.

Speaking after the accident had been reported, Chile's mining minister, Laurence Golborne, was angry. "That evacuation exit was clear for forty-eight hours after the accident, and the miners could have gotten out if the ladder had been fully in place."

There was no way out. Rescue from those above was the miners' only hope. Don Lucho and Mario Sepúlveda returned to the safest part of the mine, the refuge, to deliver the terrible news. Twenty-three hundred feet belowground, it was hot—around 95 degrees—and it was humid. The air felt heavy and hard to breathe. It was dark, too, dark as a tomb, and thirty-three men were buried alive.

WORKING TOGETHER

There was a white Nissan pickup down in the mine, among other vehicles, and Luis decided the truck would become his underground office. Strong leadership requires good organization, and from this office, Luis wasted no time in organizing the men for survival.

The thirty-three men in the mine fell naturally into two groups—the miners and the subcontractors. Each group had a different perspective on working in the mines. For the miners, it was a way of life. They knew the risks and were willing to take them every day. The subcontractors—the engineers, electricians, and mechanics, among others—were aware of the risks, but because they were not employees of the mining company, they saw their work there as temporary. Once their contracts ended, they could apply their skills to other jobs outside the mine.

When people are under a lot of stress, as these men were, differences like these can lead to conflict, and in the beginning there was tension between the miners and the subcontractors. The two groups tended to stay separate, with the miners sleeping in one area of the mine, and the subcontractors in another.

Luis Urzúa understood the importance of getting the men to overcome their differences and work together. And he knew it was vital to tell his men the truth no matter how terrifying. So Don Lucho was honest. The men might be down there for a long time. They might possibly die there. They needed to cooperate. "You just have to speak the truth and believe in democracy. Everything was voted on," Don Lucho said. "We were thirty-three men, so sixteen plus one was a majority."

In the mine, Luis Urzúa (left) and Mario Sepúlveda worked closely together. ASSOCIATED PRESS

If there was any luck on this terrible day, it was in the men's location at the time of the collapse. They were all able to reach the shelter and its store of food from where they were working. But there was not much—just enough canned tuna, peaches, milk, and crackers to last two days. Luis knew the wait for rescue would be far longer than that. Immediately, he ordered food rationing.

The air inside the refuge was full of dust after the collapse. This miner attempted to filter it with a piece of cloth over his nose. ASSOCIATED PRESS

At the beginning of their ordeal, each man was allowed two spoonfuls of tuna, a sip of milk, a bite of cracker, and a tiny morsel of canned peach a day. When it became clear that help would not come quickly, Luis cut their tiny portions of food to *every other* day.

Water, too, was scarce. Some seeped from the rock walls around them, but it wasn't much. The miners used a backhoe to dig a trench to collect what water they could. They also resorted to drinking water that was drained from the engines of the trucks. It was oily and had a terrible taste, but it was water.

EACH MAN WAS ALLOWED TWO SPOONFULS OF TUNA, A SIP OF MILK, A BITE OF CRACKER, AND A TINY MORSEL OF CANNED PEACH A DAY.

Despite the minimal amounts of food, Don Lucho asked the men to eat their meals together, and they did. Eating together helped them bond as a unit, as a family. It also served another purpose: everyone was almost starving, but by eating together, they saw that they were all getting the same amount of food.

Don Lucho organized the men into three working groups and assigned leaders. Grupo 105, named after the level where the men were trapped, was led by Raúl Bustos, a hydraulics engineer who worked on the water-supply system in the mine. Earlier in 2010, Raúl had lost his job after a major earthquake devastated the town where he was working, and he had moved north to find work in the mines in order to support his family. Grupo Rampa, the second group, took the name of the ramp, or shaft, that was the entryway into the mine. It was led by Carlos Barrios, a part-time miner who drove a taxi in his life aboveground. The third group was named Grupo Refugio, after the shelter the miners were in. Omar Reygadas, who operated a bulldozer in the mine, led this group.

The three groups of men worked eight-hour shifts, so there was activity in the mine twenty-four hours a day. Work is important to anyone, but in this desperate situation it was especially necessary. It provided something for the miners to focus on aside from their possible fate. Nevertheless, fears and worries remained. Mario Sepúlveda described the situation: "We were in total darkness. The heat was oppressive. We all felt the devil was down there with us. We prayed and prayed. It was a dark, black hole. We were buried alive. We were all so scared. We begged God to help us. We were worried we would starve to death or that the water would run out and we would die horribly from dehydration."

Despite their fears, the men continued to work. The collapse had caused a lot of debris to fall into their living area, so they cleared it away. And because there was always a danger of further collapse, the miners also worked on the roof and walls of their shelter, reinforcing them as best they could with the supplies that were on hand. By working together, the men were better able to keep hope alive and prevent despair and fear from taking over.

From his pickup-truck office, Luis called on another of his skills, topography, the art of making maps. He knew this mine well, and he carefully mapped the area where the men were trapped. There was more than a mile of tunnels and caves surrounding the 540-square-foot shelter. Luis drew a map that divided the area into working, living, and sleeping quarters. He also mapped an area for sanitation, away from the other areas, and the men went to work digging latrines. With the help of the maps, the miners were able to

A miner tries to read using only the light from his helmet. He is sitting on a roll of reinforcing mesh used to stop rocks from falling. ASSOCIATED PRESS

Edison Peña works out in the dark tunnels of the San José with only the dim headlights of a truck to light the way.
EDISON PEÑA/ADAM PATTERSON/PANOS

leave the refuge and exercise in some of the tunnels, though it was always frightening. Light became a precious commodity.

The lamps on their helmets and the headlights of the vehicles provided the only light. The helmet lamps were recharged using the batteries in the trucks. However, these batteries also supported the truck lights and needed to be recharged. This could be accomplished by running the engines, but engines need fuel, and eventually, fuel runs out. Light had to be rationed just as food was, so even with a map there was a danger of getting lost in the dark maze of the tunnels.

One miner, Edison Peña, ran in the dark tunnels anyway. Peña described running in the mine. "I was running to show that I wasn't just waiting around. I was running to be an active participant in my own salvation. I was running because I was also contributing to the struggle for our rescue," he said. Then he added, "And I wanted God to see that I really wanted to live." For Edison Peña, running, like working, was a way to keep life as normal as possible in very abnormal conditions. His running encouraged others to keep to a routine too and live as if there was a future. Whether it was running, keeping a personal journal, or writing letters to loved ones, the semblance of some kind of everyday activity helped lift the men's spirits, and optimism is important for survival.

The miners also spent a lot of time thinking of ways to communicate with the outside world. They tried the ancient technique of sending smoke signals, burning oil filters and tires in hopes of creating enough smoke to reach the surface. But fire uses up oxygen, and oxygen was scarce in the mine. And, anyway, the smoke signals didn't work.

For seventeen long days the men waited and worked, worried and prayed. Luis Urzúa counseled them with the truth. Richard Villarroel, twenty-three years old and one of the mine's mechanics, described their leader's approach: "Every day, he told us to have strength. If they find us, they find us. If not, that's that." Hunger took its toll. Villarroel said, "You just had to rough it. Every twenty-four hours eat a small piece of tuna. Nothing else. We got skinnier and skinnier . . . we were waiting for death."

> **"WE WERE IN TOTAL DARKNESS. THE HEAT WAS OPPRESSIVE. WE ALL FELT THE DEVIL WAS DOWN THERE WITH US."**

Still, as they waited, the men kept to their routine. Mario Sepúlveda said, "We knew if society broke down, we would all be doomed. Each day a different person took a bad turn. Every time that happened, we worked as a team to try to keep the morale up." Asked if he ever cried, Mario Sepúlveda was honest. "Sure. All the time. But I would walk away from the others, down a tunnel, so they would not see me weep. I knew I had to stay strong. My reputation in the

mine was as a funny guy. I had to keep that reputation going, for the sake of morale."

One of the drivers, Franklin Lobos, had played professional soccer, or football, as it is called in Chile. He said, "We pulled together when things got rough, when there was nothing, when we needed to drink water and there wasn't anything to drink. We pulled together when there was no food, when you had to eat just a teaspoon of tuna because there was nothing else. That really bonded us."

Their Roman Catholic faith also bonded most of them. As the days dragged on, Mario Gómez became their spiritual counselor, setting up a chapel area in the mine and leading the men in daily prayers for survival and rescue.

One day turned into two, then into ten, then into fifteen—more than two weeks—and there was no contact with the world above. The food had been stretched as far as it could go. It was now gone. Everyone was at the point of starvation. The men had developed skin rashes from dehydration and living in the hot, humid conditions inside the earth. Some already had medical problems, like high blood pressure and diabetes, and there was no medication in the mine to help them.

And then, at what seemed the last possible moment . . . a glorious sound! From somewhere above came the noise of drilling, drilling that meant someone was searching for them. The question was, could they be found in time?

WAITING TOGETHER

Another group of miners was at work in the San José on August 5, 2010, much closer to the surface than Don Lucho's men. Raúl Villegas was among those men. He had filled his truck with rocks and debris and was driving it up and out of the mine when he heard a loud cracking sound. On the way out, he passed Franklin Lobos and Mario Gómez, who were driving back into the mine after taking a break. He mentioned what he had heard to both men, but all of them were used to the strange sounds that often occur within a mine, and Lobos and Gómez continued downward. Moments later, a cloud of dust covered Villegas and his truck. Then, just as he saw the light at the surface, the collapse happened. "I felt an expansive wave, like when there is a dynamite explosion," he said. "The truck's engine almost went off."

Villegas emerged from the shaft. He looked back to see a huge cloud of dust pouring from the mine's opening and out into the clear desert air. Shaken, Villegas immediately reported what had happened to his manager at the San

Esteban Mining Company. Then he and a group of miners returned to the San José. José Vega was with them. His son Álex was trapped below, and he joined Villegas and the others in an attempt to enter the collapsed mine. The men drove into the mine's main access tunnel as far as they could. José had been a miner himself, and what he saw frightened him. "The floor was cracked, the ceiling was cracked, the walls were cracked. Rocks were falling from everywhere. The truth is, it was very frightening, very frightening," he said.

When they had driven in about a quarter of a mile, they had to stop. The ramp Raúl had used to drive out of the mine was now gone, crushed under 700,000 tons of rock. Though it had now been hours since Villegas had reported the accident, the San Esteban Mining Company had still not notified Chilean

Relatives of the miners comfort one another outside the San José mine as they wait for word of their loved ones' fate. ASSOCIATED PRESS

Coworkers of the trapped miners wait for word outside the mine.
ASSOCIATED PRESS

mining officials about the collapse. But word spread quickly among miners in the immediate vicinity. Some placed wooden crosses outside the entrance to a mine they believed was now a tomb. There was little else they felt they could do. Many hours later, the mining company finally informed the government of the collapse.

In Copiapó, Mario Gómez's wife, Lilianet, didn't hear of the disaster until nine that night. Her journal of that awful day reads,

> *I was waiting for him to come home from work as usual. It was just after 9:00 p.m. when the truck pulled up but it [seemed to take him a while] to come to the door. Eventually I opened the curtain and I saw it was not [my husband] but the head of operations. He told me there had been an accident at the mine. He insisted it wasn't a big deal, only a few rocks blocking the entrance, but his face told a different story.*

Lilianet's nephew offered to drive her to the mine, and she arrived later that night. For sixty-nine days and nights she remained there, not returning home even once until the ordeal was over.

After a few days passed, Ariel Ticona's young sons began to ask questions. Their mother, Elizabeth, said, "After four or five days, the children started to ask what time their daddy would come home. My oldest cried at night. The youngest, who is three, said he was going to go up there to dig through the rocks so he could get to his dad."

Rescue workers from around the world converge at the mine opening.

All of the families would have dug through the rocks if they could have. Soon friends and relatives of the other miners came to the site, joining Lilianet and Elizabeth in keeping a vigil for their husbands, fathers, sons, uncles, brothers, cousins—the men they loved. A small village sprang up. Laurence Golborne, Chile's minister of mining, had been in Ecuador when it happened, but he hurried back, arriving at the mine on August 7, two days after the accident. Rescuers had been trying to reach the miners by using heavy machinery to dig out the blocked portion of the ventilation shaft. Unfortunately, the machine's movement over the unstable mine caused the ventilation shaft to collapse too. The mining minister, discouraged, said, "That collapse meant there was no way we would make this rescue in a short period of time."

Mario Gómez's nieces Liset (left) and Martina embrace each other outside the mine that holds their uncle.
ASSOCIATED PRESS

By that point, the men had been trapped for two days. No one knew how much longer it would take to locate them or—if too much time passed—their bodies.

A plan was made to drill nine small holes, each about the circumference of a grapefruit, into the tunnels, then drop cameras through the holes in order to look and listen for the trapped miners. However, the mine's maps were out of date, and no one knew exactly where to drill. Nevertheless, the drillers began their work.

The days of difficult drilling inched by. Ten days with no word; then twelve; then fourteen. By now, the miners had been missing for two weeks, and there had been no signal from them as the various tunnels were penetrated. Dread began to edge out hope. Everyone on the surface knew food supplies had to have been exhausted, and the oxygen supply in the mine was probably giving out too. How could the men possibly still be alive?

Yet the drilling continued. The refuge was the one place that remained— the only place where the miners could possibly be. But the refuge was in the deepest part of the mine, 2,300 feet below the surface. The rock in that part of Chile is some of the hardest in the world, and it broke drill bits as though they were pieces of hard candy. It would be very tricky for the drills to reach the refuge or the surrounding tunnels, which were only fifteen feet wide. In order

31

Three of the nine drills punching holes in the San José mine, looking for signs of life. ASSOCIATED PRESS

to hit such a small target from a great distance, the drilling would have to be extremely accurate. Normally, if a drill operator was trying to hit a vein of ore, which is much wider than fifteen feet, he would have a margin of error of 10 percent one way or the other, meaning he could miss the target by 10 percent and still hit the vein. To drill through one of these narrow tunnels, the accuracy would have to be within a half of 1 percent. The miners' lives hung on that small percentage of accuracy.

On the fourteenth day, the lead drill got within one hundred feet of its target, but the hard rock caused it to veer off course. Disappointment overcame the drillers. There had been seven attempts to reach the miners, and all had failed.

Raúl Dagnino, director of one of the drilling companies, Terecem, said, "It's obviously a big disappointment for the crew . . . We normally work to find minerals. We never drilled to find lives . . . It's getting critical. More days, fewer chances."

Still, the rescue drillers didn't give up.

On August 22, at 7:15 a.m. local time, on the eighth try, one of the drills lost air pressure. It had hit an open space below. The drilling stopped, and the drillers—hardly daring to hope—thought they had heard a sound coming from below. It had been seventeen days since the cave-in, and no one really thought the miners could be alive. In the history of mining, no miner had ever been found alive after that long. Laurence Golborne was at the scene. He used a stethoscope, the same kind of instrument doctors use to amplify body sounds, to listen for any noise coming from the mine. There it was! Banging! Something was hitting the drill bit—metal against metal! A blessed, wonderful noise!

It took four hours for the drillers to pull the length of drill pipe out of the hole. When the drill bit finally reached the surface, there was another stunning surprise. Its tip had been dabbed with red paint, and two letters were attached to it. One, written by José Ojeda, said, *Estamos bien en el refugio los 33,* or "We are well in the refuge, the 33." The other was a letter from Mario Gómez to Lilianet. Translated, it read, "I'm well, thank God. I hope to get out soon. Have patience and faith. I haven't stopped thinking about you for a single moment."

At the time the amazing notes reached the surface, many of the families were eating in the common dining tent that had been set up in the small camp near the mine, a camp that now had a name—Campo Esperanza, or Camp Hope. Lilianet was in that tent, and she described the moment she found out her husband was still alive. "It was seventeen days after the accident and someone, I still don't know who it was, came running down from the mine shouting 'They're alive, they're alive!' At that moment the dining room was full of people. I had a plate of spaghetti in front of me, and we all jumped up screaming and crying. I just felt faint, dizzy, and as my eyes focused I saw the statue of the Virgin that had been placed in the corner of the tent. I went to her and kissed her dress. 'Thank you. I knew you wouldn't fail me,' I said. At that moment, I started to cry—I cried a lot. We all did. We forgot about our food and we were smiling, laughing, hugging, but still crying. We were all families of the miners, but at that moment it was like we were one family."

As quickly as possible, a miniature camera and a telephone were sent down the drill hole to the miners. Laurence Golborne was on the line at the surface, and Luis Urzúa picked up the phone when it reached him below. In a typical understatement, and with a trace of humor, Don Lucho, the shift supervisor, said, "This is the end of the shift. Luis Urzúa."

"IT WAS SEVENTEEN DAYS AFTER THE ACCIDENT AND SOMEONE CAME RUNNING DOWN FROM THE MINE SHOUTING 'THEY'RE ALIVE, THEY'RE ALIVE!'"

The minister of mines responded, and Luis added, rather simply, "We're fine—waiting to be rescued."

Joy broke out around the world. It seemed impossible, but the miners who had been feared dead were very much alive! All of them! It was Terecem, Raúl Dagnino's company, whose drill broke through to the men. He expressed the feelings of many when he said, "It is a huge miracle of God, helping us to find these miners." Most people in this deeply Roman Catholic country agreed. But the men were not free from danger, and they knew that. Franklin Lobos said, "We were never totally calm because we could still hear creaking sounds and we were not certain that we could get out. We always asked that people keep praying."

The time underground had taken a toll on their general health, and the danger of another collapse was always there. But what many had feared would be a mission to recover bodies had now become a mission to keep the miners alive while they awaited their rescue. More work, and, some said, more miracles, were needed.

Families rushed to the mine, shouting for joy at the news the miners were alive. ASSOCIATED PRESS

PLANNING TOGETHER

Luis Urzúa's primary challenge had been how to keep his men alive while they were waiting for help. He had solved that problem successfully, but now the Chilean government faced an equally daunting one: How would they get the men out of the mine?

When trying to solve problems, it's often wise to ask for some help. While the Chilean mining ministry made plans for the rescue, the Chilean space agency reached out to NASA, the United States' space agency, for advice about keeping the men healthy while they waited for a rescue that might be months away. Though NASA had no experience rescuing miners, it did have experience and expertise working with astronauts, who are often isolated from their families for months at a time in remote and challenging environments such as the International Space Station. NASA's Engineering and Safety Center, or NESC, was quick to respond to Chile's request.

NASA engineer Clint Cragg said that after receiving a call from his

supervisor about the request, "I got some engineers together and started 'what-iffing?' for scenarios in which we
might help."

Asking what-if questions is a good place to start solving
any problem. What if we did this? What if we did that?
Clint's team brainstormed what-ifs and explored potential
answers. In less than three days, they had developed plans
to help the miners.

Luis Urzúa and Mario Sepúlveda posed with some of their coworkers on September 17, 2010. A lot of planning and work remained to be done. ASSOCIATED PRESS

During the seventeen days the miners had been buried, health issues arose.
No one knew how much longer the rescue would take, so it was important to
improve the men's health as much as possible while they remained trapped
in the mine. Two medical doctors, Michael Duncan and James Polk, along with
a psychologist, Dr. Albert Holland, were part of the NASA team. Dr. Polk was
concerned, among other things, about the miners being in the dark. "We worry
about the lack of exposure to UV light, UV A and B," he said. This kind of light
occurs naturally on the earth's surface and helps kill many kinds of viruses
and harmful bacteria. But that light wasn't present below, and without it, the
miners were at high risk for fungal and bacterial infections. The men needed
doses of vitamin D, which people get naturally in sunlight, and antibiotics to
ward off infection. Also, after so long with very little food, the miners were
literally starving. Once a body is in a starvation state, it cannot accept regular
food immediately. The digestive system has to have time to recover. The NASA

doctors suggested feeding the miners a high-energy nutritional "goop" made up of glucose—a type of sugar—and vitamins for a period of time before they were allowed a more normal diet.

And of course some of them needed specific medications. Yonni Barrios had taken care of his diabetic mother when he was a child, so he was the designated doctor down below. It was his job to administer any necessary injections, take samples, conduct any medical tests the doctors on the surface might require, and report daily on the miners' health.

The NASA doctors agreed the miners had already done a lot to help themselves, and they wanted the men to continue to do that. Dr. Holland explained: "They need to be doing meaningful work. And it's important that they share the responsibility for helping extract themselves." In other words, the doctors wanted the miners to work toward solving their own problems even while others were trying to help them. This kind of effort and exercise would be good for their bodies as well as their spirits, just as it had been through the first seventeen days of their ordeal.

At the request of the Chilean navy, NESC also offered concepts for the design of the escape capsule. Using the suggestions from NESC as well as ideas of their own, the Chilean navy went to work building the capsule, which they named the Phoenix, or *Fénix* in Spanish. The

Inside the mine, the men raised the national flag of Chile in honor of Chilean Independence Day on September 18.
ASSOCIATED PRESS

phoenix is a mythical bird that lives for a thousand years. At the end of its life, it builds its own funeral pyre, jumps into the flames, and is reduced to ashes, only to be reborn. If the rescue attempt was successful, the men riding to the surface in the Phoenix capsule would certainly feel as if they were being granted new lives.

Now that the men had been discovered, two more boreholes were drilled. These three holes were used not only for communication, but to send nourishment, necessary supplies, and medicine into the mines, as well as to create ventilation. Supplies were packed into five-foot-long tubes called *palomas,* which means "doves" or "pigeons" in Spanish. Since some mining companies still use carrier pigeons to send messages in and out of mines, *palomas* was an appropriate name for the supply tubes. The boreholes were treated with a special lubricant so the *palomas* would not stick to the sides of the holes on their trips up and down the small shafts.

Dozens of *palomas* began making the one-hour trip into the mine, carrying

Clint Cragg (center) is a former U.S. Navy submarine commander. He and Dr. Michael Duncan (right of Cragg) discuss the design of the rescue capsule with engineers from the Chilean navy.
CECILIA PENAFIEL, U.S. EMBASSY IN CHILE

A food worker getting ready to insert a sandwich into a paloma.
ASSOCIATED PRESS

toothbrushes, sleeping mats, small LED lights, and games—anything that fit in a tube and might make the miners more comfortable. Perhaps less welcome were syringes for Yonni Barrios to use to administer the flu shots and other inoculations the doctors thought were necessary. Most important of all, the *palomas* carried notes and pictures from the families down to the miners, and the miners sent notes back up. Lilianet was the first family member to send a letter below. She responded to the note Mario had attached to the drill bit. "I wrote him and told him to be very patient, that we're all camped out here, following his every heartbeat. That he shouldn't become desperate, and that he try to be extremely tranquil."

The president of Chile, Sebastián Piñera, arrived at the San José, eager to talk to the miners. Luis Urzúa spoke for his men and told the president, "We hope all of Chile makes the effort so you can get us out of this hell," and President Piñera assured him, "We have made a commitment to rescue you alive." Of course no one, not even the president, was certain that promise could be kept. It might be possible to keep the men alive underground, but was it possible to raise them from their tomb beneath 2,300 feet of solid rock?

> "I WROTE HIM AND TOLD HIM TO BE VERY PATIENT, THAT WE'RE ALL CAMPED OUT HERE, FOLLOWING HIS EVERY HEARTBEAT."

LIVING TOGETHER

When word of the collapsed mine first reached them, on August 5, the miners' families came to the San José to wait, and to pray. Expecting to hear something—anything—rather quickly, they spent those first nights in the vehicles they had driven to the site. Some of the families lived in Copiapó, and in the beginning they made the hourlong drive home each night after waiting by the mine all day. Those families who lived too far away to make the daily commute spent the cold nights sleeping in their cars and trucks.

As the days wore on with no word of the men, a few tents began to spring up. Then a few more. Camp Hope took on its name. The families began erecting flags for their men, and before long thirty-two Chilean flags and one Bolivian flag, for Bolivian miner Carlos Mamani, fluttered on the hillside near the mine. Journalists from around the world began to arrive and the camp grew larger. Local charities and the Chilean government provided hot lunches and coffee not only to the miners' families, but to the journalists—an estimated 1,700 of

In Camp Hope, the family tents were separated from the tents of journalists and others by temporary black fencing material. Security patrolled regularly. Note the drills working in the background at left.
ASSOCIATED PRESS

Thirty-two Chilean flags and one Bolivian flag flew in honor of the miners.
ASSOCIATED PRESS

them, representing thirty-three countries on five continents. The world had its eye, its ear, and, most important, its heart on Camp Hope and the thirty-three men who were buried alive.

Some felt that so many writers and photographers invaded the privacy of the miners' families, who were, after all, very tired and very troubled. But Mario Gómez's thirty-year-old daughter, also named Lilianet, was at the camp, and she said, "Overall, I think they're here to help and transmit our struggle to the world. The conversations we've had around the fire have served to make us some new friends."

Friendships—new and old—sustained the worried families. There is an old expression: A burden shared is a burden halved. The families cooked together, attended church services together, watched their children play together. They even shared a birth together. On September 14, at the Copiapó clinic, Ariel Ticona's wife, Elizabeth, delivered their baby daughter. The couple had planned to name her Carolina, but from deep within the mine Ariel sent word to Elizabeth: "Tell her to change the name of our daughter to Esperanza . . . and give her a long-distance kiss." Esperanza's arrival was a new beginning not only for the Ticonas, but also for the other families at Camp Hope. The Ticona boys now had a little sister, and the birth lifted spirits and strengthened the entire camp's determination that all the miners be brought out alive.

Meanwhile, the men in the mine worried about their children and grandchildren—especially their education, which had been interrupted when the families moved to Camp Hope. In response, the government set up a school in a temporary building right in the camp. The children were given new school supplies, and with the help of their teacher, they settled into a routine of doing their lessons. They drew pictures and posted them on the walls of

Lilianet sweeping outside her tent. Translated, the sign reads: "Move forward with courage, this mountain of earth and rock can do nothing against a handful of Atacameños [*people from the Atacama*]. Strength and heart to the miners!" ASSOCIATED PRESS

Elizabeth and Ariel Ticona's baby daughter, Esperanza, arrives at Camp Hope. ASSOCIATED PRESS

their makeshift school, and they wrote notes to their fathers and other relatives in the mine. And like schoolchildren everywhere, they put on a program for their families—a celebration of Chilean Independence Day, on September 18, which that year was the 200th anniversary of the nation's birth.

The welfare of the children living in Camp Hope was on everyone's minds —including Rolando Gonzalez, a man who had been a miner himself. Known as Rolly el Payaso or Rolly the Clown, he spent weeks at the camp entertaining the children, making balloon animals, and attending birthday parties. Although he had no family in the San José, he said, "I've already done four birthday [parties] here. I look at these kids as though they were my kids."

Mario Gómez's grandson Bastian Gallardo does his lessons in school at Camp Hope.
ASSOCIATED PRESS

Marion Gallardo blows out her candles. ASSOCIATED PRESS

Marion Gallardo, Mario Gómez's granddaughter, celebrated her ninth birthday with friends and a visit from Rolly the Clown. Marion's aunt Lilianet Gómez said, "It looks like a circus around here, but it's a good kind of circus."

Life went on as normally as possible for the residents of Camp Hope. In the mine, life went on too. The trapped miners continued with their daily work duty, and the *palomas* carried letters from home and supplies to take care of the men's most basic needs. But their biggest need—getting out—had still not come close to being met. However, suggestions for the rescue were pouring in from around the world.

Ultimately, three plans were formulated: A, B, and C. All of them involved drilling a rescue shaft at least twenty-six inches across—about the diameter of a bicycle tire and just wide enough to accommodate the Phoenix rescue capsule.

Plan A would use a drill developed in South Africa, an enormous piece of machinery called the Strata 950. Only five of these drills exist in the world, and fortunately one had been leased out to Codelco, the Chilean-owned state copper company. It was being used to drill ventilation shafts at the Andina copper mine, close to Santiago. Codelco quickly transported the drill north to the San José site. An extremely accurate drill with diamond bits, the Strata 950 was placed directly above the refuge where the miners were trapped. The families at Camp Hope greeted its arrival with joy, but also with concern. The Strata 950 was very precise, but it was slow. Furthermore, the drilling process was complicated. The Strata 950 was a raise borer. This meant that first a narrow pilot hole, or guide hole, would have to be drilled down to the mine; then that hole would have to be drilled out a second time up from the bottom to accommodate the Phoenix. In essence, the hole would have to be drilled twice, and it would take a long time. The Strata 950 began drilling on August 30, 2010. It was not

THE STRATA 950 BEGAN DRILLING ON AUGUST 30, 2010. IT WAS NOT EXPECTED TO FINISH THE RESCUE SHAFT UNTIL CLOSE TO CHRISTMAS.

Miner Víctor Zamora's mother shows how letters were contained before being placed in a paloma. ASSOCIATED PRESS

47

expected to finish the rescue shaft until close to Christmas. After the initial breakthrough, Lilianet had written her husband, Mario, telling him to remain tranquil. Now it looked as if the wait would be months, and for the miners, remaining tranquil in their dark prison would be difficult.

But far away, in a small suburb of Houston, Texas, someone else was thinking about the miners and working on a plan. Greg Hall owned a company called Drillers Supply International in the town of Cypress, Texas. He had been doing business in Chile for years, and he understood the predicament the miners were in. "I would go to sleep, and I'd wake up in an hour or so just thinking about those guys sitting there in the mine, with 2,000 feet of rock above their heads . . . It really bothered me," he said. Greg began working on a plan to get them out much sooner than Christmas.

Greg Hall. ANGELICA DIAZ-HALL

Meanwhile, in Berlin, Pennsylvania, another person was thinking about the miners. Brandon Fisher ran Center Rock, Inc., a company that makes drill bits. A drill bit is the pointed part of a drill that actually bites into the ground. Another company in Pennsylvania, Schramm, made a percussion, or hammer, drill called the T130. The T130 earned its name due to its 130,000 pounds of pullback, or lifting capacity, which was particularly important in this situation. In any kind of deep drilling operation, the drill bit is attached to a round, hollow piece of steel called a drill pipe, or drill stem. As the drill bit cuts through the earth and the hole gets deeper, more lengths of drill pipe are added. Each additional piece of pipe adds to the total weight of the drilling apparatus. A

Brandon Fisher. NATASHA ZORN

hole deeper than 2,000 feet requires many lengths of heavy drill stem. Brandon Fisher and Greg Hall both felt the lifting capacity of a T130 drill was essential for this project.

Brandon was sure the combination of the T130 and his bits could get through to the miners more quickly than the Strata 950, but he didn't have any business connections in Chile. Greg Hall did. Greg said, "While designing my plan, I learned that Center Rock, Inc., in Pennsylvania was trying to sell its cluster hammer to the Chilean government to drill a large escape shaft, but no one would listen to them. I asked Center Rock to send me technical information on the hammer, and after studying its design I knew it was the final piece of the puzzle needed to perfect my plan."

At first, Brandon Fisher and Greg Hall worked independently on their plans to rescue the miners. However, Greg said, "Both Brandon and I had incorporated the Schramm T130 into our respective plans, as it was really the only drill rig available which was nominally powerful enough to accomplish the mission." Greg Hall subcontracted, or hired, Brandon Fisher's company, merged their two plans together, then presented one plan to the Chilean government. The government accepted it and called it Plan B.

Greg's plan required that one of the three lifelines—the small shafts that carried the *palomas* back and forth to the

Plan B drill on-site at the San José. The sections of orange drill pipe in the foreground will be added as the hole gets deeper. ASSOCIATED PRESS

mine—be sacrificed. Instead of being used by the *palomas,* the hole would serve as a pilot hole for the T130 drill. Not drilling a pilot hole would save precious time. Because the existing lifeline wasn't straight, however, the T130 would have to drill at an angle and widen the rescue shaft in stages. And drilling at an angle was difficult.

Because of the technical challenges of handling the T130 as it drilled an angular hole, Plan B would need the best driller in the world. Everyone in the drilling industry agreed that person was American Jeff Hart, who was then in Afghanistan, drilling water wells for the U.S. Army. Jeff was given permission to leave his post in Afghanistan, and he flew to Chile to help with the rescue.

A third option, Plan C, involved drilling first a pilot hole, then a rescue shaft, using a massive drill, the RIG-421, which is normally used to drill oil and gas wells. The RIG-421 could drill quickly, much faster than the other drills, but not with the precision of the Strata 950. Speed, however, was extremely important if the men were to be rescued in good mental and physical health. Fortunately, there was a RIG-421 already working in Iquique, Chile, about 600 miles away. The owners agreed to move it to the mine. It was taken apart for the move and its parts loaded onto forty trucks to travel to the site.

Plan A went into effect on August 30, 2010; Plan B on September 5; and Plan C began on September 19, 2010. Help was finally on the way.

"Plan your work, and work your plan" is a common expression. So is "The best-laid plans of mice and men often go awry." The first saying suggests it's good to

The drills for Plans A, B, and C all at work.
ASSOCIATED PRESS

plan, while the second warns that plans may not always work out. Both proved true as Plans A and B unfolded, before Plan C even began.

All drilling requires water to lubricate and cool the drill bit as it passes through layers of earth and rock. Without the cooling effects of the water, the friction of the drilling process would produce enough heat to melt and blunt the cutting edges of the drill bit, making it ineffective. Andre Sougarret, one of the engineers on the rescue teams, informed Luis Urzúa, "You realize that if we do it this way, there will be some 70,000 liters [18,421 gallons] of water coming down into your chamber." Don Lucho was ready. He and his men made plans to construct drainage and holding pools for the water, as well as canals to shunt it away from the men's living quarters.

Plan B drilling had gone on for only a few days when things went awry. After drilling through some of the hardest rock in the mine, the drill bit on the T130 shattered. Drilling had to stop, and the drill stem and pieces of broken bit had to be removed from the hole. Brandon Fisher said, "It's frustrating. It's not a quick process to get back out of the ground." Indeed, it took four long days to pull the drill stem out and replace the drill bit.

Meanwhile, Plan A ran into trouble. A hydraulic line in the drill began leaking fluid, and the drilling had to stop. Now both drills were silent. Below, the miners knew something was wrong. The sounds of rescue had halted. Maria Segovia, sister of Darío Segovia, had been leading daily prayers at the camp for the safety of the miners and communicating with her brother through the *palomas* on a regular basis. She spoke for her brother and the others, saying, "The boys are bad down there. The boys are bad, nervous. They can't hear the machines. They can't hear anything."

These were anxious days for the families at Camp Hope and for the miners below. They were also anxious days for the rescuers. Later Greg Hall admitted there were times when "I doubted we were going to finish the hole."

At last the T130 was back to hammering through the rock. As it hammered away, it created debris called *cuttings*. The cuttings revealed a lot about the speed of the drill. According to Greg Hall, "If you're drilling this hard rock too fast, then you get big chunks, which can cause major problems. And if you drill too slow, then you get little grindings."

Both little grindings and big chunks of rock are hard on drill bits.

The children as well as the adults worried about the miners. ASSOCIATED PRESS

Juan Andres Illanes (left) and Mario Sepúlveda examine a piece of the T130 drill that fell into the mine in a passageway 1,148 feet from the shelter. ASSOCIATED PRESS

Normally, when drilling a fresh hole, the driller can see the kinds of cuttings his drill is creating and make any necessary adjustments in the speed of the drill. However, because the pilot hole for Plan B already existed, the cuttings from the T130 drill fell into the refuge. The miners were able to help the drillers by periodically carrying samples of the cuttings to the video camera. On the surface, the drillers could see what kind of debris they were getting and adjust the drilling accordingly. Greg Hall said, "That was a tremendous advantage to us, but it also helped them help in their own rescue." In this way, the miners were able to do meaningful work, which aided in maintaining their psychological well-being, just as the NASA doctors had hoped.

REJOICING TOGETHER

At last the Strata 950's hydraulics were fixed, and it too began drilling again. Plan C's RIG-421 had been assembled and was drilling as well. All three rescue plans were finally working at once, and like the phoenix bird, hope rose in the camp once again.

And then, what everyone had waited for over the past sixty-six days finally happened. On October 9, 2010, the T130 broke into an access tunnel. Plan B had won the race to the miners.

Camp Hope went wild with joy. Church bells pealed for an hour. There was dancing, singing, and prayers of thanksgiving as adults and children celebrated together. Eight-year-old Carolina, daughter of miner Samuel Ávalos, imagined the moment when she would be reunited with the father she loved so much. "He's the most wonderful man in the world," she said. "I'm going to wrap myself around him and I'm going to rock back and forth, back and forth, like a giant swing, and I will never let him go."

Rolando "Rolly the Clown" Gonzalez—who is also a miner—joins in a confetti-strewn celebration. ASSOCIATED PRESS

Emotions run high as families await the rescue of their loved ones. ASSOCIATED PRESS.

When the drill broke through to the miners, Greg Hall and his team of rescuers did a little Chilean dance. He said, "It was just a celebration of life." Jeff Hart led an impromptu parade as the T130 was carried away from the shaft and out of the camp. Then Greg and Jeff left the camp too. Their mission had been accomplished. They felt this moment belonged to the miners' families, and they did not remain for the days of celebration that followed.

The T130 had been drilling for thirty-three days—one day for each miner. But until the last miner was on the surface, nothing was absolutely certain. There was still more work ahead and undoubtedly there was still danger. It was possible things could

In the mine, it was finally time to rejoice. ASSOCIATED PRESS

55

While waiting, Florencio Ávalos's younger son, Bruno, built his version of a mine, topped with the Chilean flag. ASSOCIATED PRESS

go very wrong, especially with the rescue shaft that had just been drilled.

The pilot hole used by Plan B's drillers was not straight; therefore the rescue shaft was not either. It had a slight bend in it—about 11 degrees. When the Phoenix capsule was inserted into the narrow rescue shaft, it would be a tight fit, with only inches of clearance. Everyone worried. Would the capsule be able to negotiate that 11-degree bend without getting stuck?

And then there was the condition of the shaft itself. The bottom portion seemed stable. It had been drilled through solid rock. But the upper portion of the shaft, before the bend, passed through far less stable earth. The movement of the rescue capsule could dislodge rocks and debris, either jamming or damaging the Phoenix. And if that were not enough to worry about, this part of northern Chile is subject to earthquakes. A decision was made to reinforce the upper part of the shaft with steel pipe. That meant more delay, more days and nights to worry and wait.

Though disappointed, the families took the news well. "We've waited two months—we can wait another two days," said Jimmy Sánchez's mother, Norma Laques. Everyone agreed. If it took a few more days to line the shaft with steel, then the families—and the men they loved—would simply have to wait.

As work to install the reinforcing pipe went on above, the miners below prepared for their rescue. They went on a special liquid diet to give them energy and prevent nausea as the capsule rotated on its way to the earth's surface. They took aspirin to thin their blood and reduce their blood pressure, which could rise due to stress and possibly cause a heart attack or stroke. They inspected the special clothing that had been sent down to them—green water-resistant coveralls, made to measure for each, since there was no room for bulky clothing in the narrow rescue capsule. The suits would keep them warm as they entered the chilly Chilean spring after leaving the stifling heat of the mine. They tried on special sunglasses designed to shield the retinas of their eyes, which had not been exposed to the sun's UV light, or even bright artificial light, for sixty-nine days.

Then it was time for more waiting, and more worrying, as each man contemplated the lonely half-hour ride to the surface of the earth.

A rescue worker displays one of the pairs of green coveralls that were sent to the miners prior to their rescue. ASSOCIATED PRESS

The Phoenix being tested before the rescues began.
ASSOCIATED PRESS

At last the winching rig that would be used to raise and lower the Phoenix was put in place over the rescue shaft.

There were test runs to be certain the Phoenix could move up and down inside the shaft and negotiate that treacherous bend. Inside, the capsule contained a bioharness that each man would wear during his ascent. The harness was designed to monitor the miners' blood pressure and other vital signs as each was winched up and out of the mine. There was an oxygen mask too, in case anyone had trouble breathing. The special helmet contained communication devices that would allow the men to stay in touch with their rescuers at all times. And finally, the Phoenix and its equipment had been designed so that each miner could put on the gear and enter the capsule unaided. After all, at the end, there would be one lone man in the mine, and he had to be able to get ready for his escape all by himself.

The excitement rose another notch as everyone prepared for Operation

Pulley System Used to Lift and Lower Capsule

The cable winds around a revolving device called a capstan, then over two pulleys, and is attached to the capsule. A motor and gears behind the capstan drive the device and control the direction the capstan turns. The direction of the turn determines whether the cable lifts or lowers the capsule.

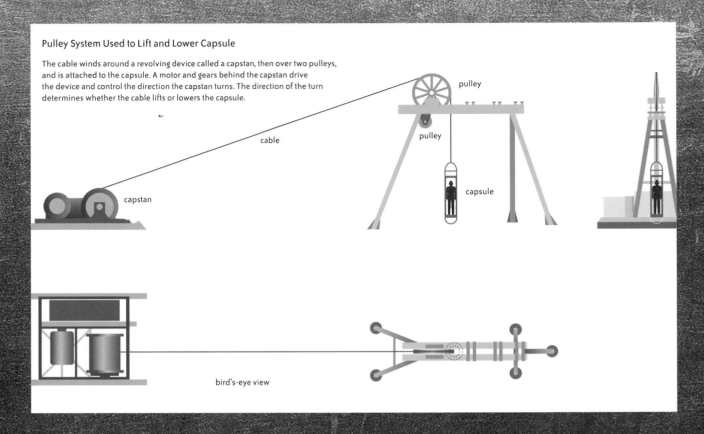

pulley

cable

pulley

capsule

capstan

bird's-eye view

Rescue Equipment

Painted in the colors of the Chilean flag, the capsule has a reinforced roof to protect the miners from rockfalls that could occur during the ascent. Levers inside the capsule would allow the bottom portion to be detached from the top, creating an escape capsule that could be lowered back into the refuge.

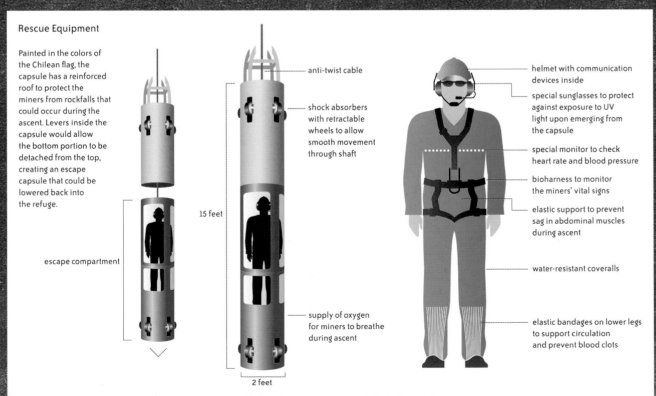

escape compartment

15 feet

2 feet

anti-twist cable

shock absorbers with retractable wheels to allow smooth movement through shaft

supply of oxygen for miners to breathe during ascent

helmet with communication devices inside

special sunglasses to protect against exposure to UV light upon emerging from the capsule

special monitor to check heart rate and blood pressure

bioharness to monitor the miners' vital signs

elastic support to prevent sag in abdominal muscles during ascent

water-resistant coveralls

elastic bandages on lower legs to support circulation and prevent blood clots

Rescue worker Manuel Gonzalez listens to final instructions before being lowered into the mine.

San Lorenzo—named after the patron saint of mining—to begin. Around the world, people crowded in front of their television sets, watching with a mixture of excitement and anxiety. No one in the camp or below in the mine was certain about anything. Because of the stress the miners were under, only three family members were allowed to greet each miner as he emerged from the capsule. Everyone else would watch the rescue on television sets that were set up all over the camp.

On Tuesday, October 12, 2010—a cold spring night in northern Chile—six rescue workers prepared to descend into the mine. Their job was to help the miners get ready for their trip to the surface. Manuel Gonzalez was the chief. An experienced rescue worker, he was employed by the mining company Codelco.

After another three-hour delay for final safety tests, it was time to prepare the miners for the rescue. Manuel moved toward the waiting Phoenix. Though the capsule had been tested in the shaft, it had not been tested with a human being onboard. He would be first. He squared his shoulders and appeared to offer a prayer, making the sign of the cross as he prepared himself. With the good wishes of President Piñera and his colleagues ringing in his ears, Manuel stepped into the capsule and strapped himself in. The great wheel of the winch began turning, and the cable was let out, lowering him into the dark shaft that led to the waiting miners. To everyone's astonishment, cameras in the mine caught the moment when the rescue capsule angled its way into what could have been the miners' burial chamber but was now a waiting room. Gonzalez stepped out and was greeted with bear hugs and back slaps. Gonzalez was the first human being other than themselves that the miners had seen or touched since they had been buried, over two months earlier.

Manuel Gonzalez (in helmet) moments after arriving at the refuge. ASSOCIATED PRESS

Five additional rescuers each took a turn in the capsule, and then the rescues began.

There was no pushing and shoving to leave first. The entire process of removing the miners had, like everything else, been carefully planned. At the suggestion of the doctors, the healthiest and most technically skilled miners would leave first. The reason? If there was a problem with the ascent, these men would be best able to communicate the issue from the capsule, and the rescuers could then attempt to fix it. And if the repair looked like it would take a while, those men had the strength to activate an escape hatch that had been built into the Phoenix, allowing the miner to go back down the shaft to wait with the others. The second group to leave would be those who were older

Emotions overcame Byron Ávalos (in blue jacket) as he waited for his father to step out of the capsule.
HUGO INFANTE/GOVERNMENT OF CHILE

Once out of the capsule, Florencio Ávalos was free to embrace his wife. ASSOCIATED PRESS

A joyous Mario Sepúlveda greets the crowd after reaching freedom. HUGO INFANTE/GOVERNMENT OF CHILE

An eager child rushes to greet Richard Villarroel, who is still in the capsule. ASSOCIATED PRESS

or had serious medical conditions. At sixty-three, Mario Gómez was among this group. The last miners to leave would have to be very strong mentally as well as physically. They had to be able to endure the long wait as each of their comrades made the ride to the surface. Like a good captain who would not leave his ship until the crew was safely off, Luis Urzúa insisted on being the last miner to leave the San José.

Florencio Ávalos had been second in command of the miners, assisting Luis Urzúa in any way he could. He also was a filmmaker of sorts and had been using a video camera sent on a *paloma* to record events below. Because he was usually behind the camera, Florencio was rarely seen in the images that reached the surface, but he was the first to be seen above. At thirty-one, he was three years older than his brother Renán, who was also trapped below and would be rescued later.

As the time drew closer, Florencio's wife and two sons arrived to wait for him. The emotion of the moment was simply too much for seven-year-old Byron, who could not hold back his tears as the winch slowly turned, pulling his father back to him. As it emerged from the earth, this metal Phoenix brought to mind the legendary phoenix rising from the ashes to new life. New life for the Ávalos family began at 12:10 a.m. At that moment Florencio Ávalos took his first breath of fresh air in sixty-nine days. Still sobbing, Byron rushed into his father's arms, followed by the other members of the Ávalos family. Sirens blew, and the crowd erupted in a cheer: *"Chi, Chi, Chi, le, le, le! Los mineros de Chile!"* All of Chile was bursting with national pride. President Piñera and his wife, First Lady Cecilia Morel, who was crying along with Byron, were waiting to greet the shy young miner, who simply said, "Thank you for transmitting your faith and hope."

Unlike Florencio Ávalos, who was more comfortable behind a camera, the second miner to be rescued, Mario Sepúlveda, was at home in front of it. He was the spokesman for the miners on the videos they made.

When Mario reached the surface he practically jumped out of the Phoenix, punching the air with his fist in sheer joy and leading the crowd in cheers. He had even brought souvenirs, a bag of rocks from within the mine, and he handed some of the rocks to President Piñera. He asked about his dog; then, a little bit later, he was more serious. "I was with God and I was with the devil; they fought for me but God won." He asked not to be treated like a celebrity. "I want you to continue treating me like Mario Antonio Sepúlveda, a worker, a miner." And then he had a bit of advice for all the people listening: he suggested that if they had an opportunity to speak with a loved one before

"THERE'S NO WAY TO DESCRIBE THE HAPPINESS OF SEEING OUR FAMILIES AGAIN, AFTER HAVING GONE THROUGH SEVENTY DAYS OF CAPTIVITY AND COMING BACK INTO THE SUNLIGHT."

Mario Gómez's first act of freedom was a prayer.
HUGO INFANTE/GOVERNMENT OF CHILE

doing something dangerous, they should do so. "Please call them," he said. "Love is the most wonderful thing that there is: the love of your parents and your family."

And so it went. The winch turned, and life returned. Life for the miners, and life for their families. Carlos Mamani from Bolivia was number four. Bolivia's president, Evo Morales, promised Carlos a job back in Bolivia and a ride home on his personal jet, but for the time being, Mamani chose to remain with the miners.

Jimmy Sánchez, at nineteen, was the youngest miner and the fifth one to reach the surface. Just a few days earlier he had sent a letter to the surface saying, "There are actually thirty-four of us because God has never left us down here."

With each ascent, the bells pealed and the traditional sirens signaling the rescue of a miner wailed in the cold night air. Lilianet and her daughters had been waiting for Mario Gómez's return to them for months, and now the time had come. Mario, who suffered from silicosis, a lung disease brought on from years of working in the mine, was the ninth miner to emerge. As Lilianet watched, Mario stepped from the capsule clutching a Chilean flag and then fell to his knees in prayer. After a moment, Lilianet rushed to him and wrapped him in her arms. Later, during an interview, Mario said, "There's no way to describe the happiness of seeing our families again, after having gone through seventy days of captivity and coming back into the sunlight. Because there were moments when we thought we would never see the daylight again."

Thirty-two miners had reached the surface, each rescue trip taking nearly an hour. Now it was Don Lucho's turn. Luis Urzúa, who had protected the miners in mind, body, and spirit during the long days underground, was the last miner to enter the Phoenix. He emerged at 9:55 in the evening on Wednesday, October 13, 2010—almost a day after rescue operations had begun. President Piñera was there to greet him with a huge embrace and several claps on the back. "I hand over my shift and I hope this never happens again," Don Lucho told an ecstatic President Piñera. "Thanks to all of Chile and to those who have cooperated. I feel proud of being a Chilean. I've delivered this shift of workers, as we agreed I would."

President Piñera replied, "I receive your shift and I congratulate you for doing your duty and coming out last. You are not the same after this, and Chile won't be the same either."

The rescuers had remained in the mine until the last miner was out. Now they emerged too. Manuel Gonzalez had been the first person to descend in the Phoenix capsule, and he was the last person to ride it out. He had spent twenty-five hours and fourteen minutes in the mine. When he greeted President Piñera at the surface, he said, "Officially, we declare this over. I am returning happy, thanks to God and all my teammates."

Luis Urzúa hands over his shift to President Piñera.
HUGO INFANTE/GOVERNMENT OF CHILE

A steel plate covers the opening to the rescue shaft. HUGO INFANTE/ GOVERNMENT OF CHILE

Each miner was whisked away to a hospital to be examined and treated. Miraculously, none seemed to have any lasting injuries or damage from illness.

Later, President Piñera placed a plate over the open mine shaft, ending the rescue, but not the story, which will be repeated whenever there is talk of how planning, working, cooperating, and praying can turn tragedy into triumph. The miners were safe, and, together, the world rejoiced.

AFTERWORD

The miners' rescue has a fairy-tale quality about it, and everyone knows that fairy tales end with "and they lived happily ever after." However, real stories do not always have fairy-tale endings.

After the San José mine collapse, Chile's government established a commission to investigate exactly what had caused the disaster. The commission found Alejandro Bohn and Marcelo Kemeny, owners of the San Esteban Mining Company, which ran the San José, guilty of not having "adequate safety measures in place." In addition to the too-short safety ladder, the commission found other violations of Chile's mine safety laws, including having insufficient supplies in the mine to properly reinforce its tunnels and galleries. The commission also found some guilt on the part of the government mining agency, Sernageomin, citing inadequate safety inspections. People within Sernageomin were immediately fired, and the agency is now reorganized.

Alejandro Bohn (right) and Marcelo Kemeny at a hearing called to investigate the mine collapse. REUTERS

In addition to its woes with the government, the mining company is facing more problems—this time, a lawsuit from the miners' families asking for millions of dollars in compensation for the men's sixty-nine-day ordeal beneath the earth. But that compensation may not happen, since Alejandro Bohn and Marcelo Kemeny have responded by declaring bankruptcy. Bankruptcy is a legal term that means a person or a company has sworn in court it has no funds to pay its financial obligations. If the court agrees, a bankrupt company may not have to repay its debts or meet its other financial obligations.

The miners have also filed a $16 million lawsuit against the Chilean government for failing to supervise the mining company properly. Miner Omar

Reygadas said they were suing not for the money, but "to set a precedent so this won't happen again. It's so conditions improve."

When the last man was pulled from the mine on October 13, 2010, they all faced a future that most assumed would be filled with endorsements, settlements, and job offers that would bring them enough money to support themselves and their families for the rest of their lives. While some of the men were paid for television interviews, and all of them were offered free trips and exciting opportunities, such as serving as grand marshals for a parade at Disney World, for the past year most of the miners have lived off the generosity of a Chilean mine owner, Leonardo Farkas. Farkas, who is not associated with the San José mine, gave each man 5 million pesos (about $10,950) and a motorcycle, and doubled that amount for Ariel Ticona's family because of the birth of Esperanza.

For many of the men, that money is now gone. It has been reported that Claudio Yañez and Pedro Cortez have sold their motorcycles for food. According to Chilean newspaper *El Mercurio,* fifteen of the miners are now unemployed, three are selling fruits and vegetables on the street, two are running small grocery stores, and four men have returned to the mines. Among the unemployed are men who are too psychologically damaged from their ordeal beneath the earth to return to work.

Still, there are bright spots. Luis Urzúa and six others have become professional motivational speakers. Mario Sepúlveda has formed a consulting business and travels around Chile and other countries, offering his services. On August 5, 2011, the one-year anniversary of the mine collapse, he accompanied the Chilean foreign minister Alfredo Moreno to Washington, D.C., for the opening of a Smithsonian Institution exhibit on the dramatic rescue at the San José mine.

And while a few of the men have returned to the mines, Mario Gómez will not. He made a promise to Lilianet, and he is keeping it. He and Lilianet are going to take time to enjoy their children and grandchildren. She and Mario have been married for more than thirty years, and Lilianet talked about the notes they sent each other through the *palomas,* exclaiming, "Imagine,

Their long separation is over, and Lilianet and Mario are together again. HUGO INFANTE/ GOVERNMENT OF CHILE

exchanging love letters after all these years!" Later, as she contemplated their future together, she said, "I realize that the man I'm getting back is not the same Mario. God has given us the opportunity to restart life. It's a new beginning, an opportunity. It's a miracle."

Miracle comes from a Latin word that means "to look on with astonishment." Certainly everyone who participated in this rescue effort, and everyone who watched around the world, looked on in astonishment. Now, despite the problems the men may face, their rescue seems miraculous in all senses of that word. And miracles are the best "happily ever after" of all.

THE THIRTY-THREE

Left to right: (top row) Carlos Mamani, José Ojeda, José Herriquez, Luis Urzúa, Omar Reygadas, Mario Gómez, Pablo Rojas, Claudio Yañez, Juan Illanes, Mario Sepúlveda, Juan Carlos Aguilar

(middle row) Yonni Barrios, Víctor Zamora, Carlos Barrios, Víctor Segovia, Claudio Acuña, Carlos Bugueño, Ariel Ticona, Samuel Ávalos, Renán Ávalos, Darío Segovia, Richard Villarroel

(bottom row) Ósman Araya, Jorge Galleguillos, Jimmy Sánchez, Franklin Lobos, Florencio Ávalos, Esteban Rojas, Raúl Bustos, Pedro Cortez, Daniel Herrera, Edison Peña, Álex Vega

THE RESCUERS
IN ORDER OF THEIR DESCENT INTO THE MINE

Manuel Gonzalez, Roberto Ríos, Patricio Robledo, Jorge Bustamante, Patricio Sepúlveda, Pedro Rivero

GLOSSARY

Antibiotics: A form of medicine used to prevent the growth of bacteria and other disease-causing organisms.

Ascend: To rise or move upward.

Backhoe: An excavating machine with a hinged bucket attached to a rigid boom. It digs by drawing the bucket back toward the machine.

Borehole: A hole made with a drill.

Cuttings: The scrap pieces removed from a hole as it is drilled.

Dehydration: A state in which not enough water is in the body.

Descend: To move downward.

Diabetes: A disease in which the body is not able to regulate levels of sugar (glucose) in the blood. Treating diabetes often requires regular doses of insulin.

Dragline: A machine that hauls in a bucket attached by cables.

Drill: A machine or tool with a shaft and a bit that is turned at a high rate of speed to make a hole.

Drill bit: A tool that fits into the drill and cuts to make a hole.

Driller: Someone who operates a drill.

Drill stem: A tubular extension to the drill bit; also called a drill pipe.

Economy: A system of production, distribution, and consumption of goods, services, and wealth.

High blood pressure: A condition in which the blood passes through the vessels at abnormally high pressure, causing stress on the heart and other organs. Also known as hypertension.

Hydraulics: A form of engineering that uses the motion of fluid to drive machines.

Latrine: A designated area, usually outdoors, that is used as a toilet.

LED light: Light-emitting diode; a type of light that uses small amounts of energy.

Margin of error: The amount of acceptable deviation or movement away from a specific target. The smaller the margin of error, the more accurate the work must be.

Mine: A deep excavation in the earth that contains minerals.

Miner: A person who extracts ore from a mine.

Mineral: A substance formed in the earth that is not animal or vegetation.

Mining: The process of extracting minerals from the earth.

Ore: A rock or mineral from which a valuable substance, like copper or gold, can be extracted.

Psychologist: A doctor trained to understand the mind and emotions.

Pullback: A drilling term that describes the lifting capacity of a drill.

Refuge: A place that protects from danger.

Retina: The part of the eye, located at the back and inside of the eyeball, that senses light and color.

Shaft: A deep passage into the earth.

Shaft mining: A method of mining where a deep, vertical tunnel is used to extract deposits of ore.

Shift: A regular time period when people work.

Starvation: A state in which the body lacks enough food to survive.

Subcontractor: A secondary company often hired to do specialized work for another company.

Surface mining: A method of mining where minerals are extracted from shallow deposits of ore.

Topography: The art of exact representation of a particular place, as in mapmaking.

UV light: Short waves of invisible radiation that occur naturally in sunlight.

Vein: A layer of ore in a mass of rock.

Ventilation shaft: A small shaft used to allow air to enter a closed area.

Weeping: A mining term that refers to the sounds of an unstable mine.

Winch: A machine that pulls or lifts objects using a rope or cable wound around a drum.

'VE been inside mines. I've visited gold mines in Colorado, salt mines in Texas, coal mines in Pennsylvania. I know how scary it can be when you are deep inside the earth and someone turns out the lights, as one tour guide did. There is no darkness like that. You are just wrapped in black. Of course, my visits inside mines were just that—visits. I was a tourist, not a miner. Yet I've never forgotten my experience, so perhaps that is why the story of the Chilean miners resonated so strongly for me. And I wasn't the only one who felt this way. When news broke that thirty-three men had been buried alive inside the San José mine, the whole world seemed to respond in a deeply emotional way.

As I followed the daily reports on television and in the papers, the early news seemed to indicate that these men—like so many other miners before them—would not survive. Though my heart ached for them and their families, I thought that would be the end of their story. And then there was hope! The men had been found *alive* after seventeen agonizing days in the dark. Just like a good piece of fiction, this true story had taken a fascinating twist. By the time the rescue was under way on October 12, 2010, I was glued to my television set, watching every moment. I knew I wanted to tell this extraordinary story. But Houston, Texas, is a long way from Copiapó, Chile, and now the miners were out of the mine and refusing to talk. So how does an author put together an authentic story without access to the miners themselves? It was a daunting question.

A quick Internet search provided access to the articles written by journalists from around the world who had traveled to Chile to cover the story. That was a relief, because now I had access to the reports of eyewitnesses. I also watched television specials on the miners. I took notes, but I was happy to see that transcripts from television shows, like *NOVA*'s October 26, 2010, show, "Emergency Mine Rescue" (www. pbs.org/wgbh/nova/tech/emergency-mine-rescue.html), were available to me. And I wasn't limited to news reports from the United States. Half a world away, *Carte Blanche*, a news magazine TV show, airs in South Africa and other countries throughout that continent. On October 17, 2010, *Carte Blanche* presented a program on the disaster called "Chilean Miners." That show and its transcript are available at beta.mnet. co.za/carteblanche/Article.aspx?Id=4161&Showid=1.

Closer to home, the *PBS NewsHour* interviewed driller Greg Hall on October 26, 2010. (www.pbs.org/ newshour/bb/weather/july-dec10/chilean2_10-26.html?print). *NOVA* also interviewed Greg (www.pbs. org/wgbh/nova/tech/hall-chile-au.html) on October 27. Of course, I read both those transcripts, but the best news came when I realized that Greg's company, Drillers Supply International, was located in a suburb of Houston, my home. So I was able to interview Greg myself.

A team from NASA headed by Clint Cragg went to Chile to consult with the Chilean government about preparing the miners for the long wait for rescue. You can read some of the same information I read at www.nasa.gov/news/cragg.html.

Though the miners sent word that they would not talk to the news media, it is human nature to talk, and soon some of their comments began to appear. See "Freed Chilean Miner Mario Sepúlveda Reveals Darkest Days" from the Telegraph Media Group in London (www.telegraph.co.uk/news/worldnews/southamerica/ chile/8069092/PIX-AND-PUBLISH-Freed-miner-reveals-darkest-days.html) and Jocelyn M. Richard's AOL News article, "Chilean Miners Rescued: In Their Own Words" (www.aolnews.com/2010/10/13/chilean- miners-in-their-own-words/). Mario Gómez spoke to reporter Annie Murphy from National Public Radio on October 18, 2010. Read that story at www.npr.org/templates/story/story.php?storyId=130639040.

The miners' families spoke out, too. Reporter Fiona Govan talked to Lilianet Ramirez, the wife of Mario Gómez, and filed her report, "Chile Miner Rescue: A Wife's Story" in the *Telegraph* on October 12, 2010 (www. telegraph.co.uk/news/worldnews/southamerica/chile/8060004/Chile-miner-rescue-a-wifes-story.html). Lilianet also spoke to Andrew Gregory of the British newspaper the *Mirror* on August 26, 2010. That report, "Wife of Trapped Chilean Miner Mario Gómez Speaks Out" can be found here: www.mirror.co.uk/news/ top-stories/2010/08/26/wife-of-trapped-chilean-miner-mario-gomez-speaks-out-115875-22514081/.

I played treasure hunt on the Internet, as each source led me to another one. I found mistakes, and I was careful to note who was providing the information I was reading and verify facts against several sources.

Indeed, as a small example, I found Lilianet's name also spelled as Lilliana and Lilian. Since "Lilianet" was the spelling that appeared most often, that is the spelling I chose to use. Byron Ávalos's little brother, Bruno, was often identified as Byron in photographs. It took some detective work to be certain I had the right name for the photo of him building a replica of the mine that held his father.

On October 12, 2010, ABC News reporter John Quinones filed a video report on the reaction of Arlen Yanez to seeing a televised picture of her father, buried in the mine. You can watch her reaction at abcnews.go.com/WNT/video/children-miners-wait-fathers-11865185. For more on the miners' children, read Adam Patterson's article from October 15, 2010, "Me, the Chilean Miners, and Their Children" at www.viceland.com/wp/2010/10/me-the-chilean-miners-and-their-children/. Wikipedia is a good source for general background information. Their account of what happened at the San José mine can be found here: en.wikipedia.org/wiki/2010_Copiap%C3%B3_mining_accident. Anyone can contribute information to Wikipedia, so if you choose to use this resource for a report, verify the information provided against the sources listed at the end of the article.

Authors always like to use books as jumping-off points. Yet at the time I was writing, no books had been published on what had happened at the San José mine. I was forced to research most of my information in newspapers, on television reports, and on the Internet. I have included several more websites I used in the section "For Further Reading." However, if I were to list every article I read on every site, these notes could be longer than the book itself! Websites can disappear, and their content can change. But as this book went to press, all of the websites I have mentioned were still up and running. Plus, there are now some good books on the subject as well.

Finally, I drew on my own experience of being inside a dark mine when the lights went out. I was in darkness for only a few minutes, but it terrified me. I used those memories to imagine what it must have been like for these thirty-three men as they endured their imprisonment for sixty-nine days. As I read, thought, and wrote about the miners, I was grateful for their freedom, and appreciative in a new way of my own.

Elaine Scott

For Further Reading

Aronson, Marc. *Trapped: How the World Rescued 33 Miners from 2,000 Feet Below the Chilean Desert.* New York: Atheneum, 2011.

Bartoletti, Susan Campbell. *Growing Up in Coal Country.* Boston: Houghton Mifflin, 1996.

Burgan, Michael. *Chile (Enchantment of the World, Second).* Danbury, Conn.: Children's Press, 2009.

Hyde, Natalie. *Life in a Mining Community.* New York: Crabtree, 2009.

Morrison, Marion. *Chile (Countries Around the World).* Mankato, Minn.: Capstone Heinemann-Raintree, 2011.

These books, written for adults, were published after I wrote my book:

Franklin, Jonathan. *33 Men: Inside the Miraculous Survival and Dramatic Rescue of the Chilean Miners.* New York: Putnam, 2011.

Pino, Manuel. *Buried Alive: The True Story of the Chilean Mining Disaster and the Extraordinary Rescue at Camp Hope.* Foreword by Natalie Morales. New York: Palgrave Macmillan, 2011.

Additional Websites of Interest

BBC News. "Jubilation as Chile Mine Rescue Ends." October 14, 2010. www.bbc.co.uk/news/world-latin-america-11539182.

Barrionuevo, Alexi. "Carnival Air Fills Chilean Camp as Miners' Rescue Nears." *New York Times*, October 10, 2010. www.nytimes.com/2010/10/11/world/americas/11chile.html.

Howland, Jack. "Chilean Miners Survive by Diligent Food Rationing." August 25, 2010. blog.utc.edu/TheLoop/2010/08/25/6994/.

Kamlet, Lee. "While 33 Chilean Miners Wait Below, True Hope from Above." September 14, 2010. abcnews.go.com/International/wife-trapped-chilean-miner-birth/story?id=11638317.

Katersky, Aaron. "Chilean Miner Edison Pena Arrives at NYC Marathon." November 4, 2010. abcnews.go.com/US/chilean-miner-edison-pena-arrives-nyc-marathon/story?id=12059804.

Long, Gideon. "New Challenge for Chile's Rescued Miners." October 21, 2010. www.bbc.co.uk/news/world-latin-america-11593012.

Nowak, Mark. "Los 33 (Short Biographies of the 33 Miners in Chile)." October 10, 2010. coalmountain.wordpress.com/2010/10/10/los-33-short-biographies-of-the-33-miners-in-chile/.

Walsh, Ed. "Why American Drilling Hero Jeff Hart Will Not Be at Chile Mine for Miners' Rescue." www.examiner.com/sf-in-san-francisco/why-american-drilling-hero-jeff-hart-will-not-be-at-chile-mine-for-miners-rescue.

Webber, Jude. "Last of 33 Trapped Miners Is Rescued." October 13, 2010. www.ft.com/intl/cms/s/0/064dbdf2-d6ee-11df-aaab-00144feabdc0.html#axzz1SPEJnOmF.

Webley, Kayla. "How the Trapped Chilean Miners Survived on Limited Supplies." August 24, 2010. www.time.com/time/world/article/0,8599,2013137,00.html.

Page numbers in **bold type** refer to photos and their captions.